T0066908

TEN PROVERBS SINGLES SHOULD KNOW BEFORE MARRIAGE

The Real Truth about Singleness and Marriage and What the Church Will Not Tell You

Lucinda G. Graham

WESTBOW°
PRESS
A DIVISION OF THOMAS NELSON
& ZONDERVAN

Copyright © 2015 Lucinda G. Graham.

All rights reserved. No part of this book may be used or reproduced by any means, graphic, electronic, or mechanical, including photocopying, recording, taping or by any information storage retrieval system without the written permission of the publisher except in the case of brief quotations embodied in critical articles and reviews.

Scripture quotations taken from the Holy Bible, New Living Translation, Copyright © 1996, 2004. Used by permission of Tyndale House Publishers, Inc., Wheaton, Illinois 60189. All rights reserved.

Scripture taken from the King James Version of the Bible.

New Revised Standard Version Bible, copyright © 1989, Division of Christian Education of the National Council of the Churches of Christ in the United States of America. Used by permission. All rights reserved.

WestBow Press books may be ordered through booksellers or by contacting:

WestBow Press
A Division of Thomas Nelson & Zondervan
1663 Liberty Drive
Bloomington, IN 47403
www.westbowpress.com
1 (866) 928-1240

Because of the dynamic nature of the Internet, any web addresses or links contained in this book may have changed since publication and may no longer be valid. The views expressed in this work are solely those of the author and do not necessarily reflect the views of the publisher, and the publisher hereby disclaims any responsibility for them.

Any people depicted in stock imagery provided by Thinkstock are models, and such images are being used for illustrative purposes only. Certain stock imagery © Thinkstock.

ISBN: 978-1-4908-7544-6 (sc)
ISBN: 978-1-4908-7546-0 (hc)
ISBN: 978-1-4908-7545-3 (e)

Library of Congress Control Number: 2015905179

Print information available on the last page.

WestBow Press rev. date: 4/23/2015

To all the people who have supported the ministry
God has given me, your prayers, time, love,
and finances did not go unnoticed. Bless you!

CONTENTS

ACKNOWLEDGMENTS

I thank God for the experience to share my story with others who are wondering about marriage and what to expect. I would like to thank my students for allowing me to practice the Word of God on them. Without the practice, I would not have seen the manifestation of the Holy Spirit at work. I would like to thank my friends far and near who witnessed my pain and perhaps felt my pain but never once judged me. My family has always thought I was over the top. Thanks for encouraging me to express who I am and to never give up. I would like to acknowledge my daughter Hope.

PREFACE

The shelves are lined with princess dolls and bridal dolls, which adds to the fantasy of one day being married to Prince Charming or Mr. Right. This is normal because it's every girl's dream to be married with children. There are sitcoms and family television shows pivoting a twisted view of what marriage and life are really about. But the reality is that there is no Prince Charming or Mr. Right who will sweep you off your feet. Prince Charming is a television mogul illusion, and Mr. Right can be wrong for you if you are not very careful.

Mr. Right may say all the right things and make all the right moves, but has Mr. Right shared with you his dark side? Prince Charming may pay for the elaborate gifts and fine dining experiences, but has Prince Charming shared with you that his financial status is insolvent? Mr. Right and Prince Charming both have a past. The question is this: Are you equipped mentally and spiritually to handle the past? What really happens during the courtship? Is it really a courtship? What is the difference between dating and courting?

As I write this book, I think of the women who cried on my shoulder when they realized their marriages were over. I filed for divorce five years before my divorce was finalized. There are ten things I wish I had known as a single woman before I got married. I decided to share the proverbs and the reality of my marriage in a book. In this book I will refer to my ex-husband as Jay-Jay.

I bought tapes and books on how to live single and holy, but nothing compared to real life. I purchased marriage preparation materials and found that after the honeymoon I was not prepared for marriage at all. I believed scripture in the literal sense that I was a help meet, so I did whatever I could to make sure his dreams became reality. I purchased a truck for him and I even put his business in my name. This was done in the name of love because I believed marriage was until death would do us part, not divorce. I learned that Mr. Right was the wrong man for me.

America's divorce rate is extremely high, and there is no explanation, only theories. Theories are only good for classrooms and textbooks. I was listening to a morning show and heard a marriage expert say that "marriage is not work." I have read and have heard of the extreme measures married couples take to keep their marriage together. Yet it still fails. I just have to believe, as a minister of the gospel of Jesus Christ, that marriage is not for everyone and that some of us just need to remain single.

This explains the title of my book *Ten Proverbs Singles should know before marriage.* Marriage is not for everyone, and neither is remaining single; however, you have to be faithful in either singleness or marriage. I have forgiven myself and my ex-husband and have moved on to greater things in life; therefore, I am not bitter. I let go of the past and the strongholds that came with divorce, and I allowed God to redefine me and refresh me for a new and prosperous future.

As a divorcee, I would like to share my feelings during the time when I realized my marriage was over. I realized my marriage was over when my spouse moved from the master bedroom with me to the guest bedroom to sleep alone. I realized my marriage was over when we stopped courting me and began arguing with me. I realized my marriage was over when my spouse would come home after midnight. I realized my marriage was over when my spouse began degrading and belittling me, especially my ministry.

When I realized divorce was imminent for me, I felt as if divorce deemed me a failure and, as a minister, a hypocrite. Divorce did not give me the option of feeling secure because insecurities entered and left me desolate and isolated. Divorce also left me feeling abandoned and rejected. These are similar to feelings that I had as a single person going through a breakup, but with a divorce, the feelings were amplified because there are labels.

The labels of divorce are initiated by the Enemy (Satan), but divorce is rebuked by the church and the biblical Scriptures. I remember completing an application and the options for my marital status were these: married, divorced, single, or widowed. I began thinking, *Now why should one know if I have been married and now divorced?* I selected the single option because I am single. The hurt and pain of a divorce leaves a scar. The statistical labels and religious dogma are scars.

If you have never encountered pain, go through a divorce. It leaves a feeling of brokenness. This is why a single female should remain single and maintain her sanity because the hurt and pain is too unbearable. The same goes for males; however, I cannot relate to the hurt and pain of a man because men handle every situation differently. Even though the old adage tells us that time heals all wounds, no one wants to be wounded, abandoned, or rejected. There are other reasons why you should remain single and not marry hastily. You should understand the ten proverbs before you get married, and then you will be in a better situation than most who have been married for decades and are miserable.

Decide if you want to be married for the sake of being married! Decide if you want to be in a committed relationship! Decide if you want to be married to join forces with a partner to gain financial stability! Decide if you want to be married because you are in love and would like to be with this person until death do you part! Making a decision about marriage now while you are single is very significant to the conclusion of your life story as it relates to marriage.

I challenge you to read and meditate upon each chapter of this book with an open heart and mind to allow the Holy Spirit to speak to you. Your life is not a game and should not be played with by someone who is playing games or just going through the motions of life. I have heard men say, "I married her because she begged me to marry her." "I married her because her daddy made me marry her." Be happy in your marriage. If you decide marriage is for you, be committed to your spouse and treat your spouse with love, respect, and adoration.

Chapter 1

SAVE AND INVEST

Next came the servant who had received
the two bags of gold, with the report, Sir
you gave me two bags of gold to invest,
and I have doubled the amount.
—Matthew 25:22 NLT

When I met my ex-husband, I was a recent divinity graduate. I had spent my inheritance on living expenses as well as on books, supplies, and other essentials. I did not have much money when I returned home, so I sought ordination in the church to provide a salary/income. I began working with the campus ministry at the local university. The salary was not much for a person with a dual master's degree, and I had to do the job of a secretary, administrative assistant, project manager, etc. as I did not have a secretary or an assistant. I did not understand how to develop and structure a board of directors, so I funded much of the daily operations so the campus ministry could flourish. I was not thinking about marriage, children, or myself when I accepted the position and began ministering on a college campus, surrounded by economically challenged students in an area considered disadvantaged. Please note that the students were bright students with potential but were labeled because of the socioeconomic status in the rural area.

I engulfed myself in the ministry, sowing and tithing both time and finances. I was not saving 10 percent of my income. I was basically throwing money away to living expenses, shopping, and generous giving. I did not have a mortgage, rent, or a car note because my dad before his passing had purchased a car for me and I was living in his house. Therefore, there was no reason I shouldn't have had a substantial amount of savings put away for a rainy day. Financial literacy was not functional at this point in my life.

Ministry was essential, and applying the principles of tithing and sowing was the only financial understanding I had acquired at this point. I was shopping so much in the area, that I scheduled a meeting with my colleague at the time that I met my ex-husband. (For the sake of identity purposes, as stated earlier, I will call my ex-husband Jay-Jay.) I was leaving the mall when Jay-Jay called out to me for my telephone number. I dismissed him with a business card that specified that I was a minister. In the past my business cards were a deterrent for men.

Jay-Jay called my home phone for months before I returned his numerous calls. I was not impressed with his persistence. Actually I was irritated and disgusted with the way he approached me at the mall, but I managed to return his phone calls. When I began conversing with him, I decided he was sweet and kind. Jay-Jay felt it was time to have dinner. Sure enough, he flashed a luxury vehicle, high-end restaurant, and the gift of gab he obviously inherited from fraud phonics, but it worked on this tough evangelist from a small town. He shared with me that he had no children and was financially secure.

Dismissing all the gifts of discernment and allowing all the gifts of materialism to surface, I believed his biographical monologue and politely shared with him that I was not interested in continuing the relationship with him. Needless to say, the night ended, but his phone calls continued. Six months later he bought me a 3.2-carat engagement ring. We were married. Many were happy for me. Others were speculative, and some were jealous. I was confused.

I decided to share the excitement of my engagement by hosting an engagement dinner during the summer at the banquet hall of an exquisite restaurant. The arrangement was for each of us to invite twenty-five close family members and friends so they could become acquainted with one another. I invited twenty-five, and he invited fifty. The money I managed to save for six months was completely splurged on an elaborate celebration in which people spoke negatively about us as a couple, many voicing their lack of faith in our longevity. Except for his sister and uncle, I never saw the fifty people he invited to the engagement dinner during the entire three years of our marriage.

After the engagement dinner I decided the wedding would be a private ceremony with only twenty people attending. The wedding was beautifully decorated, and there was enough food for two hundred people. It stormed. There was a thunderstorm warning the entire day, and it felt as if the storm hit the building. I was surprised the electricity remained on during the ceremony and reception because of the thunderstorm and tornadic activity. The ceremony was over, and we were off to the Caribbean, for our honeymoon.

The wedding gifts were minimal—four hundred dollars and a photo frame. It was obvious my wedding was not a commemorative event. I did not know it at the time, but our family did not believe in us or our marriage. No one ever bothered to share this information with me, however, until I filed for divorce. The financial cost for the engagement dinner, the wedding, and the honeymoon were a stretch for me because Jay-Jay did not offer to pay for anything. It was his belief it was the woman's expense. The truth was Jay-Jay did not have any money.

Jay-Jay called everyone in his cell phone directory to inform them that he was traveling to the Caribbean for his honeymoon. He was convinced that the rain on our wedding day meant showers of blessings and that the lack of smiles on our guests' faces was due to their economic hardships. He also used economic hardships as the reason why we did not receive more gifts. I was more concerned that this marriage was a gig and not a relationship or partnership. Teamwork was eliminated from his vocabulary, and every expense was charged to my credit card. I wondered what in the world had I gotten myself into.

The honeymoon was great, and the Carribean was beautiful. Now it was time to start working, saving, and paying bills, but only one person was getting dressed each morning and going to work—me. Finally after three weeks I asked Jay-Jay why he was not working and what was going on. He explained he was a contractor and the jobs were seasonal. I explained to him that was nonsense because road construction was daily. This is when I learned he lacked the license, bonding, and insurance to do the necessary work to maintain his phony lifestyle.

I suggested that perhaps we could live off his savings while he waited to take the licensure exam and begin working. He didn't have any savings because he lived flamboyantly, taking care of his immediate family and his five children by four different women. Two of these women were his former wives. Reasons number five and six should help demonstrate how important it is to learn all you can about someone before you determine if the person is the right one or the wrong one. This is why I had to write this book. I needed to share this message with singles and especially Christian singles who are living in a bubble. I was really struggling to save money because now I had an added expense and additional liabilities.

You should save and invest for your future whether you decide to marry or not. Having money in the bank and not in your pocket is better than being broke. Having income other than your monthly or weekly paycheck will help you gain financial security. A wise old man use to say, "Money may not be everything, but it sure helps." Even the Scriptures attest that "a party gives laughter, and wine gives happiness, and money gives everything" (Ecclesiastes 10:19 NLT).

Saving and investing will give you confidence in who you are and security in who you allow to come into your life. Because I was financially distressed, I became vulnerable. Being vulnerable to a predator was not beneficial to my future or to my well-being. Single people should always save and invest. Before I went to theology school, I was investing in the stock market and did not have student loans or credit card debt. I was independent and not interested in dating or partying because I was earning money without working. Then the stock market crashed, and I lost a great deal of my investments.

Somehow I became distracted and lost the vision of saving and investing. Do not lose the vision of saving and investing into your future. If you decide to date or marry, do not splurge your finances to impress someone. A girlfriend of mine used to tell me, "A new broom sweeps well for the first three months." What she was saying to me was that I needed to be aware because people will put on a façade to become whoever they need to be at that moment to impress me, but in three months the real person would surface. Be natural and allow God to be in control of your relationship.

As a single person having financial control, the only purpose to being married would be to continue the financial control or to share the wealth. Perhaps the person is not as financially aware (like-minded or equally yoked) as you. Then what will happen to the marriage? The finances will disappear first and next the marriage. Once a person's mind-set is changed to equate to yours, then marriages can work, and finances can be made. However, if the person has a poverty mentality of "make the money and spend the finances," then you will never get ahead as a married couple.

A single person has more opportunities for acquiring wealth because it is only your life and your finances at risk. A single person has no one to consult concerning joint finances or joint business ventures. A single person can awaken one morning with an idea and go make it happen. The only person to consult would be God. A single person does not have to make decisions for two people or a family.

Allow me to define my personal definition of a single person. A single person is an individual who is not married and does not have a partner or a roommate. A single person is an independent-minded and independent-living person who is making decisions without the consultation or approval of a spouse or partner. In layman's terms, a single person is a person who lives alone and only consults with God and makes decision based on his or her intuition. A single person is also a strong-willed and strong-minded individual with a dream, vision, purpose, and goals ready to be accomplished.

Saving and investing is important to your future as a married person or as a successful individual. Marrying before the proper time is a disaster, and it will take a strong person to weather the storm. Marrying the wrong person is worse than being cut with any object. Marriage is a serious matter. Most marriages succeed because the two minds are alike and their goals and vision for the future are similar.

Most marriages succeed because the couples become one another's cheerleaders. One is encouraging the other, and the other is advancing the unit. There is no division in a successful marriage. Both married individuals are committed to each other, the vows, and the vision for the future. Teams are successful because someone followed the plays and used intuition, when needed, to make the plays and win the games.

Likewise, in a marriage it is a team effort, and the cheerleader role is played by both spouses. The plays are played until the game is complete and victory is evident. Selfishness and one minded roles are not essential to marriages. Marriage takes work, vision, and effort. If you are not a team player, then marriage is not for you. If you have a one-sided vision to see only yourself succeed, then stay single.

If you have a one-sided vision to see only yourself succeed, then you are indeed a bachelor or bachelorette. You should not waste anyone's time on the phone, social network, or Internet. You should not waste people's time by taking them to dinner for dates unless you are upfront in letting them know you are just requiring their presence for the evening only. Be honest with yourself and with people. Stop playing games and save and invest your money.

Save and invest is the first proverb for this book because no one wants a broke man or woman. To be honest, a broke man cannot take care of a family. There is an exception—if there is an agreement or if that is the card life dealt—that the man will take care of the children while the woman goes to work. What if that is not the case? Then who wants a financially insecure man or woman in their life, someone not contributing to the household living expenses? This is why both single men and single women should save and invest their money before marriage.

Save and invest is the first chapter for this book because money is essential to a better quality of life. Money gives everything according to the biblical text; therefore, save and invest for your future. Even if you decide to marry, make sure you have finances available for the first three years of marriage, which are the most trying and challenging times in a marriage. You may marry a rich person. That would be great. But have your own money, even if it is not much. Make an effort to save and invest, stop spending frivolously, and start making wise investments.

I was told by a man once that a woman with her own house and money is intimidating to a man because a man needs to feel that he can contribute something. I have never understood how men think, and I probably never will because I felt that his opinion was lame. A man can always contribute something to a relationship and to a marriage regardless of whether the woman is independent with financial securities. The more, the merrier! Bring your finances on over for more investments. The utility bills are due every month. If there was an additional income, then perhaps the female could save her portion of the utility bill for next year's investment on rental property.

I shared earlier that each partner should be a cheerleader to encourage each other to make the *play* to achieve the common goal. Leave your egos at mom's house because two are always better than one. I am not talking about only a physical two but a spiritual and mental two as well. When two people work together, you can achieve so much more. When I was married and was working the business with my husband, we accomplished so much until his jealous, *hood* friends starting telling him he was the man and I needed to be under him.

This is when I became just a figurehead in the company and the secretary became the face for the company. The secretary was his eye candy in the office. When you get married, it is best to end the relationship with the hood friends and the ego because these two will cause a lot of problems in a marriage. The same can be applied to a woman. The club girls are no longer your buddies, and the guy with the alternative lifestyle whom you divulge all your business to will have to go as well. It is time to think like a team and work as if you are leaving a legacy to twelve children and thirty grandchildren.

The era when men were supposed to take care of the women and women were supposed to sit at home and cook has ended. Both parties should bring something to the table for coherent distribution and financial equality. Some men will have those types of insecurities and will not embrace women's independence. There are those men who will not have insecurities and will want women to take care of them. Single women stay single before you take care of grown men.

Single women, make investments for your future and save for your financial security and comfort. These are challenging and trying times where everyone will have to work together to bring something to the table as it relates to marriage. Saving and investing is the most crucial element for this era. Wining and dining, spending and lying around is for someone else, but for those who are about making things happen, I encourage you to save and invest. Pray and seek God concerning investments and use wisdom. Stop procrastinating and get moving!

Single men, make investments for your future or your future wife and family. Go forth and make a deal today that will change the course of your life forever. This is not the time to hang out with the boys to collect cool points when opportunity is knocking. Open the door. Welcome and embrace new ideas for saving money and investing money. I encourage you to pray and seek God for your next investment and financial endeavor.

Saving and investing is the number-one proverb you need to know before you get married, and it is the number-one reason that may keep you married. If you do not have savings or any investments, then stay single. If you are single and have savings and investments, stay single and continue to build on those investments. Marriage has its place and will happen in God's timing, but right now save and invest all you can. Save and invest in your future to become financially secure and financially stable.

Chapter 2

STAY TRUE TO YOURSELF

Don't copy the behavior and customs of this
world, but let God transform you into a new
person by changing the way you think.
—Romans 12:2

After our first date Jay-Jay told his best friend about me, and his
friend wanted to take us to the seafood buffet at the casino. I do
not like casinos and decided I would not enter the doors again, not
even to eat. I informed Jay-Jay of my vow and thought he would
suggest another restaurant, but he did not. When I met Jay-Jay at
his town house to meet his friend, to my surprise, we were going
in the direction of the casino. I expressed my disgust and asked to
be taken back to my car.

He tried to convince me that casinos are fine because churches
have events at the casinos and because he had seen church buses
parked in the parking lot. I understood his persuasive argument,
but he did not respect my belief or my decision to not patronize

the casino. He called his friend on the phone and told him my belief, and his friend laughed and asked to speak with me so that he could convince me further. My thinking through all of this was that I am going to delete Jay-Jay from my life forever because he has no respect for my personal spiritual belief as it relates to casinos. Ultimately I decided to indulge the couple who was highly anticipating meeting me.

Jay-Jay's friend and his spouse were friendly and assured me they were devout Christians who eat at the casino all the time because the casino prepared the best buffet around. My thought was that they did not know if I was a recovering gambler or a recovering addict, and it seemed as if they did not care as long as they were able to size me up. While we were at the dinner table, Jay-Jay's friend winked and threw kisses at me. He was asked to stop with the gestures, and he ignored the requests. Jay-Jay did not rebuke his friend, which I found odd.

After dinner I asked Jay-Jay whether he noticed that his friend was flirting with me. Jay-Jay informed me that he saw the entire performance and thought I was enjoying it because I never asked him to stop. I was appalled and shocked at the nerve of this man to insult my intelligence with this foolishness after he disrespected me by taking me to a casino to eat. I did not respond any further after I got back to my car. The night ended, and I went home. I did not respond to any of his phone calls. Nor did I initiate any phone calls. His phone calls were constant, and many of the voice messages he left were accusations that I wanted his friend and not him.

I possessed common sense and believed something was wrong with this man, and I should have had every number disconnected and changed because he was someone I did not need to know. I should have immediately dismissed him, but I did not. He convinced me that he was sorry for insisting I go to dinner with his friend, and he apologized for not stopping the game his friend persuaded him to play on me. He told me his friend believed my silence was a sign that I wanted the flirting to continue and that I enjoyed the attention. I really did not enjoy any of the night at the casino and should not have compromised my beliefs, and stayed true to myself.

When you are in a relationship, staying true to yourself is important to hold dear to your heart—and it is proverb number two—because there will be situations and circumstances that place you in an uncompromising position. The key is to stay true to yourself and your beliefs. If not, you will fall for anything, which is what I did. The adage is this: "If you don't stand for something, you will fall for anything," and during this situation I did not stand for something. I did not pass the test, and I did not adhere to the signs and wonders God graciously placed before me that night at the casino. Since that incident, I have witnessed married men confront other men for disrespecting their wives, looking at them unabashedly, or touching them inappropriately.

Never compromise your morals, your beliefs, or your stance on a particular issue. Always stand up for yourself. Not taking a stand for myself that night showed Jay-Jay signs of weakness, and because I lacked financial stability, there was vulnerability there as well. For example, when an individual is confident and secure about a thing, they are very dogmatic about defending it or guarding it. However, if there is a weakness or an open door, anything goes.

Had I been financially secure, I would have dictated the restaurant and demanded respect that day and the days to follow. As I look back at the situation, I realize that today that I am a different person. I am more secure and mature. I learned from my insecurity and will stay true to myself. When something happens one time, as a creature of habit, I am determined not to feel that way again. I felt defeated that night, and I was humiliated. I was insulted and angry, and I felt like there was nothing I could do about it.

I could have stayed true to myself and the beliefs that I possessed, and I would not have allowed the manipulation and deceitful tactics to get the best of me. Staying true meant I would not have conformed to the standards of Jay-Jay's world and would have demanded Jay-Jay conform to the world in which I held dear and true to my heart. In the end, I settled for less and not for the best. I settled for what I thought was security when I should have possessed my own financial security. I lacked the security and maturity to confront these men.

It took me three years to heal from the wounds, hurts, and feelings of guilt I encountered because of Jay-Jay. I am expressing my emotions honestly with the intent of relating and thus understanding that the self-blame and the guilt were released once I forgave myself. God gives us room to make mistakes so that we can be chastised or corrected. I am grateful to a loving God who cares and understands. I am especially grateful because God knows humanity's heart and is able to deal with every emotion and feeling.

In any relationship, whether it is business or personal, you must stay true to yourself. Do not allow yourself to play a role that is out of character. Be yourself and be confident in handling every situation and every problem. It is easy to change characters to impress others, particularly in a relationship when feelings and emotions are expressed. Know who you are and know that you possess the power within you to do and be who you want to be; therefore, conforming to another's standards is not necessary.

I have seen women become Cinderella once they are in a dating relationship; however, months prior they were the wicked stepsisters. Before I married Jay-Jay, I was contemplating dating an attorney who knew that I was a minister and spent a lot of time ministering and praying for people. One day he decided we needed to have a special talk. In the event we got married, he did not want to come home and have a living room full of women praying and preaching the gospel. I could have easily told him that I would be a good little housewife, but I did not tell him those words. What I told him was that whomever I chose to marry, our home will become what God wants our home to become.

I respected his need to share that with me, but I also knew that me as a minister would probably be problematic. The truth was that he had insulted me. Scripture would state that he had caused an offense. He did not understand who I was as a person or as a minister. This conversation occurred before I applied, and I was accepted into theology school.

I can truly say that theology school was a life-changing event and I was never the same person after theology school. I became open to every belief but never the notion that all gods were the same. There is only one God who rose and predicted His death in the Holy Scripture, and no one was going to change that theory. I learned that many felt speaking in tongues was repulsive, however, I did not feel that way and continued to speak and pray in my heavenly language. Any gift from God is not repulsive and should be utilized to the fullest.

In theology school there were many young students entering the program with immoral lifestyles, yet they were pastors, church leaders, and saints. There were many confused about their own relationships with God and did not understand the authority and power of the Creator, God. I thought it should have been easy, but then I realized it was about a personal relationship with God. It was about repenting/turning from sin and accepting Jesus Christ as Lord and Savior. The relationship with Jesus was the most challenging act for many theology students.

Even though theology school did not extinguish the flames of the fiery gospel within, the flames seemed to diminish after graduation when I met Jay-Jay. Jay-Jay's theology was about numbers and making people feel good after a message. My theology was hellfire and brimstone. My favorite statement was this: "If you don't repent and get yourself together before you die, in hell you shall lift up your eyes." Jay-Jay convinced me that I would never get students to come to the campus ministry with that message. Jay-Jay assured me that students needed to hear of God's love and forgiveness.

Jay-Jay convinced me, therefore, I preached a message of God's love and forgiveness, and I was losing students by the dozens. Jay-Jay constantly assured me that all was well and that I was doing a great job. As I reflect over the time Jay-Jay stated those words to me, I can hear sarcasm in his voice. I had compromised my integrity and the gospel message to please a man. I knew what was right in the sight of God but chose to do otherwise.

Jay-Jay used the ministry God had given me to manipulate me. He also took advantage of my kindness. When people discover your weakness, they take advantage of you until they have gained complete control. My weakness was a desire to see the campus ministry succeed with an increase in student participation and funding. The students were excited about the fire and brimstone messages. I learned later that they wanted to hear those messages to keep them from doing wrong. I also later learned from others that Jay-Jay was propositioning a few of the female students, which is why most did not return.

My focus and attention was in the wrong area, and I should have focused on what God wanted for the campus ministry and not Jay-Jay's flesh. I should not have altered my beliefs or lifestyle to please Jay-Jay's flesh. Stay true to yourself because if your partner wants you to change something that is beneficial to God, that could only mean your partner dislikes you. To dislike one part of you is to dislike all of you. If your partner sees where they can change one thing about you, they will constantly work on changing other things that could compromise your integrity.

If you did not want a nose job or breast implants before you met Mr. Right or Mr. Wrong, I can assure you that you do not need them now. As individuals, we need to realize that we are not puppets or dolls that can be altered to appease our partners. If the individual is not what you want, then move on to the next person and stop trying to change the individual to the puppet or doll you desire to create. We are certainly grateful for corrective criticism. For example, if one thinks a female should try a red lip gloss instead of a brown lip gloss that is acceptable. However, commenting that one's lips are too small and may need enlargement means that individual should find another creation to recreate. You are not the one.

Receive compliments from people with a simple thank-you. You do not have to explain where you purchased the outfit from or how you derived the item that was complimented. Act confident and secure, even if you don't feel like you are. You do not have to be a doormat or a punching bag for someone to love you and adore you. It has to start with the individual. Stay true to yourself and exercise your right as a human being. As God's creation, you are fearfully, beautifully, and wonderfully made.

Chapter 3

AVOID NEGATIVITY
AND BE POSITIVE

So also, the tongue is a small thing, but
what enormous damage it can do.
—James 3:5 NLT

If you ever decide to get married, begin speaking positive words over your marriage. Speak positive about marriage, speak positive about dating, speak positive about finances, etc. Sometimes humanity speaks with negativity because of a fear of the unknown, particularly when there is doubt, disbelief, or a lack of assurance. No one wants to be around someone who is negative all the time. Sometimes a person would like positive surroundings to uplift and encourage. Negativity damages beliefs, dreams, and visions, but positivity encourages, motivates, and drives.

I remember during marriage counseling the pastor told us that if we save for rainy days, then there will be rainy days. It is fear that allows one to speak negatively by making statements such as, "I will save for a rainy day in the event he or she messes up. Then I will have some money." Negative statements like these feed and breed into a marriage, thus creating mistrust from the very beginning. I agree with investing and saving not for a rainy day but because it is the right thing to do for yourself and your family. Save for sunny days, such as vacations, honeymoons, and wedding anniversaries.

People say things because they think it is cute or makes them seem wise, but if you listen to the words that come from most people's mouths, you will be in disbelief. Before I got married, married people would always tell me, "Do not get married." These same married people would not expound on the statement but would always say it with passion. I often wonder why so many married people tell single people not to get married. Is it because they do not want single, independent individuals to struggle or go through pain? I really believe it is because of some negative thought or negative seed planted on the inside that causes one to react.

I share this book on ten proverbs singles should know before marriage with you because I want you to take a look at yourself before you bring another person into your life. If you have a life of pain and hurt, then marriage is not going to cure or heal you. As I stated in the previous chapter, marriage is not for selfish people because each will have to make many sacrifices in order to make the marriage succeed. It is selfish to bring someone into your life or into your space, knowing that there are unresolved issues from a past relationship or childhood. Marriage is not a cure for hurt.

If you are divorced and feel that the second, third, or fourth time will be a charm, then you are feeding into negativity. Divorce only takes one time and for some unknown cause, maybe twice, but three and above are signs that serious counseling and healing is needed. Divorce is very painful. I wrote an article once detailing why God hates divorce, and my belief was that it is painful emotionally, financially, and physically.

It is painful emotionally because you feel rejected, abandoned, and depressed. The emotional pain leads to physical problems, such as weight gain, high blood pressure, weight loss, and/or anemia. The emotional and physical pain leads to financial pain because there is time off from work, which results in limited income. The lawyer fees are astronomical, which can lead to financial debt. Divorce is not favorable to either party because both parties are emotionally, financially, and physically drained by the system. There is a court fee, attorney fee, alimony payments, child support payments, and the list goes on and on.

The question is this: Who wins? Stay single if you think that you will just file for a divorce if the relationship doesn't work. This is not a game or some new toy for Christmas that you can play with during the holiday and then place in the corner to play with later. There is a human being, a human heart, and a human mind involved when it comes to marriage. What God has joined together, let no one separate. Not even the parties involved should separate what God has joined together.

God hates divorce because God doesn't want humanity to hurt. Marriage begins with a union, and divorce ends with abandonment. Divorce is a negative word, and I try not to use it when I am discussing marriage with struggling couples. It should *not* be an option. Talk positively in your relationships. Encourage your mate.

I spent a large sum of money during my divorce because my emotions were all over the place. I did not realize that lawyers had patience and would do anything necessary to find extra money to charge the client. I paid a criminal attorney to defend me for criminal charges my ex-husband filed against me. I paid three divorce lawyers because I felt that the lawyer was either too slow, or was using my case to barter with other attorneys for other cases unrelated to me or were in cahoots to see who could get the most money at the end of the divorce.

I was emotionally, financially, and physically drained. I thought I was going to lose my mind during the entire divorce process, but I had to constantly speak positively. I would say that I would not let this divorce affect my weight, my mind, or my finances. I would meet negative people every day who would offer negative wisdom, and I would rebuke the negativity openly or under my breath. The Enemy feeds on negativity and continues to hurt God's people and makes the people of God feel useless.

People of God have to realize their worth and understand who they are as children of God. We have to talk right and speak positively at all times because any negativity will feed the seed within. We are valuable stock for the kingdom of God, and we have to understand that if we are joint heirs, then there should not be any negativity in our vocabulary. Your mate may speak mean and ugly things to you, but you can turn those words into positive words. Simply say, "I do not receive that. That is unacceptable." These types of positive statements will make a person stop and think.

Positive words work. As a campus minister, I have encountered many students, but this one particular female had issues of hurt, rejection, and abandonment because she was adopted. She was always negative during choir rehearsal or just sitting around and chatting. I shared with the choir director a vision that God had given me for the weekly services, and she immediately stated that it would fail. I simply said to her, "I do not receive that because the Word of God says, 'Write the vision, make it plain, (Habakkuk 2:2 KJV) and to speak those things as though they were.'"

She rolled and batted her eyes and later became inactive with the campus ministry. I was not mean or rude to her by any means. It was the Word of God that pierced the negativity within her. When you have negative people around you, you have to stay positive by using the Word of God and meditating on the Word daily. You have to think positively even when you see negativity.

In the small town where I grew up, there is an enormity of negativity to feed any seed within. But after I developed, received, and maintained a relationship with God, I began to speak positive. I spoke to a group of youth about knowing their worth in Christ. I explained to them that when you know your worth, negativity will not stop you from flourishing and prospering. That is the Word that I leave with you for this chapter. When you know your worth, negativity will not invade your thoughts, heart, or mouth. Even when the potholes are overtaking the roads and the cats are leaving dead rats on your doorsteps, continue to speak positive words over your situation. When you know your worth, positive words are easy to speak in any given situation.

Chapter 4

KEEP IT TO YOURSELF

> Don't talk too much, for it fosters sin.
> Be sensible and turnoff the flow!
> —Proverbs 10:19 NLT

Women have a natural gift of talking, and sometimes we can talk too much. We want the man in our life to know everything. We especially want them to know how the last men we dated hurt us and took off with the cleanup woman. Well, that is not always a great thing to do. Telling a man too much can backfire.

All the times I have dated a man, I never heard him share with me about the orgies he had or the number of women he slept with in his lifetime. Those are like trump cards, and you do not share that card until you know beyond a shadow of a doubt that she is not the one you will marry. Women are opposite from men in this regard. Sometimes we like to boast when really we should just keep quiet. We like to show that we are definitely marriage material when we should just be ourselves.

Before I got married, a young lady I had deemed as my friend began stalking me and defaming my character in the community. Well, Jay-Jay was in my life at the time, and she was not fond of him, because she felt as if he was using me. She was right in that he was using me, but she did not handle the situation in a discreet or amicable manner. One day Jay-Jay said to me that the young lady was a lesbian because she wanted me as her lover and was angry that I had selected a man instead of her. I laughed because I thought it was the most ridiculous thing I had ever heard.

The young lady was not a lesbian. Neither was I. She was hurting because she felt she was losing her friend. We shopped together, went to church together, and shared secrets like friends do. She knew that our friendship would be strained if I married this man. She needed someone she could trust, and she found that person in me. Close friends are not always lesbians.

One day Jay-Jay and I argued about him spending too much money. Suddenly I heard him utter the words that I was an undercover lesbian. I stopped the conversation and did not speak to him for a week. I realized that I was grateful I did not share anything with him about my past because it would have been used against me. I am not in favor of giving too much information about my past.

Men can be the most selfish and inconsiderate people on the planet. Most men are usually insensitive about weight issues as they relate to women. Men will tell their significant others that they are beautiful just the way they are. Then moments later that same man is caught looking at a smaller, younger, or more attractive woman. This type of action hurts a woman emotionally.

Telling a man you need to lose weight is the same as ordering a pizza, frying potatoes in lard, adding three cups of sugar to eight ounces of punch, and then eating and drinking it all. Essentially it will do more harm than good.

Inconsiderate and selfish are just two of the characteristics of most men I have encountered that I wish to share at this point, but there are several others that define the characteristic of men perfectly. At the university I served initially, I proposed a challenge for the full-figured ladies to lose weight. One of the ladies purchased her packet but was not interested in working out. She understood that losing weight was essential to her health and vitality, but there was something hindering her from working out. I knew that it was spiritual, but she was not confiding in me.

The gentleman that I had advising me on the project would call every day. One particular day the man called and asked how the ladies were working out. I told him about the one lady who was slow with her effort, but with persistence she would come around. This gentleman became extreme and demanding. His concern became dictating and domineering. I told him that in my opinion the young lady obviously had emotional issues and that she was aware she needed to lose weight but that her weight was considered a form of protection.

His comments about the young lady helped me to understand that there is more to a person than what meets the eye. A person can be aware of his or her need for help, but because of a personal struggle or hindrance, the response can be delayed. Sometimes men fail to see the underlying reason or motive behind a situation. Most men sometimes miss the obvious, thus creating offenses, wounds, and insults in the woman's life. Most men need to be more sensitive to the needs of a woman.

Because of most men's insensitivity, I would advise women to just keep personal details about their lives to themselves. Sharing case-sensitive information with the opposite sex may be used against you in vulnerable and heated situations. Sharing sexual details about past relationships is very unwise and unhealthy. Men may be very gracious to share with you how they slept with thirty-five women in one night and danced for bachelorette parties, but you should keep quiet. Airing your dirty laundry is not a competition in which you can expect to win a prize, because the only prize you will receive later is ridicule and insults.

I have conversed with men who are older than fifty and like to brag about how they were promiscuous. I am sorry! I do not want to marry a man who has slept with the town and community. There are some spirits I just do not want to go to bed with, and thirty-five women with their thirty-five lovers would equate to seventy people. Thanks but no thanks! Jesus paid the price on Calvary, and breaking additional soul ties is not a habit I would like to have. Therefore, men bragging to me about the numerous women they have encountered are not impressive. It is scary!

Women keep many emotions bottled inside because of their fears of rejection and failure. So when we meet men who show just a minimal amount of interest, we get all excited and bubbly. We decide we want to share our secrets and pour out our hearts to this new godsend because we have never felt like this before. We as women began to think that this person had to be the man we have waited for, and then we began pouring out everything. We think in this silence he cares and he understands. To think that he cares is foolish. He is just gathering information to use against you at a later date.

The information he gathers will be used later to control you. The information gathered is used later to belittle you. The information is used later to elevate him and degrade you. He will make himself appear to be Moses or Jesus because you will not hear much about his past, but he will know all about your past, your faults, your fears, and your failures. This is when you begin to second-guess who you are and question your worth.

You had never felt so empty or worthless until you met Mr. Wrong, with whom you shared all your secrets. Now he can make a sarcastic remark about your past every time you dress nice or achieve a promotion on the job. Never discuss your past with a man, particularly with a man you are interested in marrying. Some men need edification and gratification, and your nasty past will help with boosting their egos. Just keep your business to yourself. If you need to talk to someone, go in your closet and talk to God. God is always listening.

Men remember what they want to remember. They may forget your first kiss. They may forget your first date. They may even forget to order you roses for Valentine's Day, but they will not forget your secrets. If your secrets are juicy and bubbly, you can expect to hear them again when he is angry or sad.

When I refer to men in this chapter, I am speaking of men as potential spouses, not best male friends or gossip partners. The best male friend and gossip partner are different when it comes to sharing information because they just want to hear the juicy gossip and size you up in their minds. A potential mate, however, will make sure that you are aware that your past is not behind you because the information you shared with him will be available for recapitulation at a later date. I hate to be the bearer of bad news, but sharing too much information with a potential mate is damaging and detrimental to the relationship. Whenever in doubt, keep it to yourself!

I would like to offer a caveat here. When I use the term *men* or *male* in this book, I am not referring to all men. I am only referring to insecure men or men with unresolved hurts. I have met couples who have been married for thirty or fifty years, and the people in those relationships are still in love with each other. However, there are those couples who have been married thirty or fifty years and who are miserable. Not all men are like the men I speak of in this book, but please understand they are out there.

Chapter 5

SPEAK UP. I CAN'T HEAR YOU.

Avoid profane chatter, for it will lead
people into more and more impiety, and
their talk will spread like gangrene.
—2 Timothy 2:16 NRSV

Ladies, chapter 5 and 6 are very important and very vital to the life and vitality of any relationship. Communication in a relationship is instrumental. I cannot hear what you are saying if you are not talking. I will not know your likes or dislikes if you do not tell me. A prime example is the Holy Bible. The Creator makes His likes as well as His dislikes explicit in the Bible because He wants humanity to have a full relationship with Him. The Holy Bible coupled with the Holy Spirit is the Creator's tool of communication for humanity. You cannot go astray in your relationship with God.

Likewise in a secular relationship, communication is the only way to know a person's likes or dislikes. Communication is the only way to know if a person is telling the truth or a lie. You must ask questions. You must start conversations to gain information that will prevent you from being hurt, deceived, or used later in the relationship. I ask that you not ignore the signs. Let me give you several examples before I move on.

There was a very attractive young lady who was single. She was constantly bombarded with requests for dinner dates or just phone conversations. She told me this story about a man who visited her job. He was clean-cut and muscular, and he smelled very clean and drove a luxury sports car. She began asking him questions about himself, as she did not see a wedding band on his finger. The conversation was short because he had to return to work. He just wanted her to know that he was thinking about her.

As days went by, she told me how she constantly drilled him with questions about his past, his childhood, his present, etc. This man called her inquiries interrogations. The phone calls diminished. One day he asked her to meet him for lunch, and she agreed; however, right before the actual lunch date he made an excuse. The same thing happened constantly with public outings, but not when he wanted to visit her place or when he needed a place to stay. She brought these things to his attention, and not to her surprise he was married.

Of course, he said the marriage was an arrangement for the two children. His wife was having an affair with her coworker, and the list of excuses went on and on. This man's lack of conversation earlier told her he was hiding something. His evasiveness of public places with her told her he belonged to someone else. His willingness to come to her home and spend time with her told her that he was just playing a game and that he was in it for one thing. Married men have the same profile. It does not matter where they live or work.

Married men are never available when you need them. Married men make excuses about everything, especially when they are distributing money. The amount is never what you need but what they want to give you. Married men never stop at one woman. They keep going until they get caught, if they ever get caught. It is a game because they have not grown up and settled into the marriage God gave them. Not all married men are cheaters, but to know if you are engaging one (a married man), start talking.

King Solomon gives instructions to the reader about adultery. He talks about the other woman in Proverbs 5 as being a danger. I especially admire verse 15 when he encourages the readers to drink water out of their own cisterns and running water out of their own wells. This is the best advice one man can give to another. I believe if men and women would respect the sacred vows of marriage, then adulterous affairs would be limited or not committed.

Another example of why conversation is important in any relationship is because it really saves you from future pain and heartache. While I was dating Jay-Jay, I noticed photographs of little children everywhere in his condo. I asked who the little boys were, and he told me that they were his nephews. I could see the photos were old, which meant the boys were probably much older than the photo projected. I began asking about his children. He told me he did not have any children. Jay-Jay lied because I learned he had an eighteen year old daughter whom he had just met.

It is almost an honor for a single woman to meet a single black man with no children, and I thought the same about Jay-Jay.

I found out later the boys were actually Jay-Jay's sons and the daughter had been in his life since birth not when she was eighteen years old. I did not ask enough questions. I did not ask about his involvement in the boys' lives.

There were so many questions I could have asked that would have triggered a conversation and would have led to the truth. I did not ask how he got so attached to his nephews to have their photographs line the wall in his townhome. I did not ask which sister was the mother of each child in the photograph. I did not ask when I would meet these boys. When I did find out the truth, the trust in the relationship was broken, and when I wanted out, I was blackmailed and threaten.

When a new person comes into your life, ask questions about his school days. Talk to people you know from his hometown about him. When you ask the question, people will began giving you additional information you did not ask for. I remember after I filed for divorce from Jay-Jay, his second ex-wife told me how her story was so similar to my own story. I remember thinking, *If I had known, I could have asked her to share her story back then.*

Some ex-wives will tell you the truth, and there are some who will paint a horror story; however, I believe your conscience and your God will direct you to know the truth. I would not hesitate to talk with an ex-wife should I begin a new relationship. There are people who know stories that you are not aware of and will gladly share the stories. I remember my mom telling me a woman called her a week before my wedding and told her a lot of negative things about Jay-Jay, but she did not share the information with me because she felt it would have hurt me and she did not know if it was the truth. Almost six years later after a bitter divorce, three arrests, jail time, and an absent parent, I wish she would have let me made the decision whether the woman had spoken the truth or it was just tall tales.

I agree with the Scriptures that say there are some vain conversations we should not engage (2 Timothy 2:16 KJV) ourselves in, but there are those conversations that will edify us. Do not keep quiet about something that involves your future. If the relationship is serious and you are three months into the relationship, start talking. Ask questions and do not blink your eyes or dismiss something that did not set well with you. If you think that something else should have been said or if chills run up your spine in a bad way or goose bumps crawl up your arms, then you need to investigate, not dismiss these feelings of intuition.

These are signs that something is not right. My sister always says, "If your stomach begins to rumble with a nervousness or sickness, *run!*" Conversations should make you feel peaceful and not eerie once you leave. You should not be in a daze after a conversation, trying to put the pieces to a puzzle together. Having a conversation is like digesting food. It should not be painful.

This is real life, not a fairy tale or a television sitcom. Your tears are real. Your heartaches are serious, and your mental well-being is precious. Do not avoid this truth because it will save you from pain and heartache. Verbal abuse, physical abuse, and mental abuse can be detected in a conversation. Regardless of whether you witness the conversation or the conversation involves you, the truth is in the conversation. Go after it!

Chapter 6

THAT IS NOT A RHETORICAL QUESTION

I will question you, and you shall declare to me.
—Job 38:3b NRSV

There is nothing wrong with asking questions when you want answers. Asking questions is not a sign of insecurity as one man in my past stated to me. One can ask questions without nagging or probing. One can also ask questions in a respectful manner, discerning what is confidential and what is disrespectful. There are those questions that are purposefully avoided.

There are those questions that need answers, and answers are needed right away. Seldom will a woman find a man who is a talker. Most men are quiet and passive. They are low key and do not want a lot of drama. When you do ask a question, most men will not answer, particularly when the question involves admission to a wrong.

Most men would like women to think they never do wrong, and the same principle applies to women. As a woman, I do not want to be caught doing any wrong. I want to always appear perfect, even though I have imperfections, but I do not want my male counterpart to detect that weakness. The same goes for a man. He does not want any weakness on display, particularly when he is trying his very best to impress. This is why it has to be clear that any question you ask is not rhetorical.

You are expecting an answer to the question. If you do not expect an answer, you will never get an answer. It is just that simple. You will have to guess, and that is not fun because your guess could be right or could easily be wrong. I have to admit that I jump to too many conclusions and later find out I was wrong.

This is why rhetorical questions are not acceptable in a relationship. You will need an answer to the question you are asking. You will want peace in every relationship, and not having answers to your questions will not bring peace in the relationship. Leaving conversations unresolved or open is not healthy and only leads to constant aggravation later on in the relationship. Nothing should be left to one's imagination, especially if there is an answer to a question or an explanation warranted. Keep a level head and remember to ask God for thick skin when you are dealing with questions in relationships because you never know what you may hear.

Remember that verbal and physical abuse is not positive in a relationship. If you ask a question and seconds later someone calls you a derogatory name, then this is a sure sign that this is not the relationship for you. Conversations should be candid, friendly, and open. Therefore, if the conversation is opposite of friendly and open, remove yourself immediately because that person has issues. A person with issues is not good for a relationship.

In my opinion, unresolved issues are cycles that are used to destroy the mental and psychological fortitude of a person. People with unresolved issues like to put others down and make others seem small while they appear intelligent. However, you are diminished, and it seems you are of less or no value in the conversation. These types of issues can lead to fights. Fights can lead to beatings, and beatings can lead to death. Everyone wants a compliment even on a bad hair day. So avoid negative relationships that will only foster abusive and profane language.

Ask questions and declare your answers. Do not let someone walk away from you without answering a question that may be crucial to the future of your relationship. Be careful in how you present the question. Always avoid *why* because that puts even the best of us on defense. Remember, asking questions helps to determine if this person is Mr. Right or Mr. Wrong. Asking questions is not a bad thing. It is a great thing to do. Make sure when you ask your questions, you get the answers you deserve.

Chapter 7

STOP BLINKING

Don't get sidetracked; keep your
feet from following evil.
—Proverbs 4:27 NLT

Do not overlook anything in a conversation, a letter, or a gesture. Do not close your eyes to things that cause you to raise your eyebrows. If something was done to startle you or raise concern or suspicion, then it probably is a concern. If the moral character is strange from one situation to the next situation, then you have reason to be concerned. These things will not change in the marriage.

If you do not like it now, then it will only heighten or be amplified in the marriage. If the tone of the conversation in private is obnoxious and the tone of the conversation changes when you are around guests, then you have an actor in your troupe. I used to say teaching was acting, but now I see that too many people in dating relationships are acting. The couple is acting as if they are in a dramatization, depicting characters who are only fitting for the relationship. Once the relationship is over, the stage play is over, and you see other people come forth, people you never knew.

I remember dating this guy, and during the three months of dating I never heard him curse or act rudely toward me. I decided to end the relationship amicably; however, when I saw him months later, he called me every profane word he could think of, and he was very loud and disrespectful. A year later I met a young lady who knew the guy. I asked her about him, and she told me he was crazy. She continued by saying, "You never know who he will be from one day to the next day." I felt as if something was not right with him, and I thank God I realized this soon enough.

It is the little things that add up to much, according to my father. I never understood that until I got married. It was the little nerve-picking things that I noticed when we were dating that got on my nerves when we got married. But I blinked because of the dazzling gifts. I am not sure if I thought I could change him once we got married, but if I did think it, I was proven wrong quickly.

I have a girlfriend who told me that when she was in prayer one day, the Holy Spirit spoke and told her not to trust men not to love them, and not to expect anything from them. She told me she knew God was talking about men because she asked God in a previous prayer why she was always hurt after a relationship ended. She was twice divorced and could not find a commitment from any of the men she dated. I believed what she heard came from God because God loves His daughters and is not happy when we hurt. I often wondered whether the message the Holy Spirit spoke to her is for single women only.

I know that men are hurt by women in relationships as well, but I believe if there are statistics out there, it would show women are hurt in relationships more than men. We watch the movies of how young girls are molested and then prostituted because of their lack of worth. I have been told stories of how parents sell young girls to men just to make ends meet. Women with abusive pasts look for attention from the wrong men. Most of our men with absent mothers look for attention from the wrong woman. Healing is needed for those who are hurting.

There are no straight and narrows to anything in life, especially relationships, with the exception of heaven. We often second-guess ourselves when we discern things that we are not comfortable with. We often ask self too many questions and gather several second opinions before we dismiss the thought. We often think we are judging when we are actually discerning. Many of our answers to the questions were right before our eyes, but we blinked, thinking we shouldn't be too harsh.

It is our future that is at stake, and we should take every precaution before we make any final decisions. The signs were there, but they were ignored. The sickening feeling in your stomach was there, but you ignored it. The hair stood straight up on your arm, and the chills raced up and down your arm; however, you still ignored the signs for whatever reason. Now we must live with the consequences of our actions.

There is always forgiveness and redemption in every act. I will share my prayers and testimonials in chapter 10, which addresses forgiveness. Life is too precious to blink at white lies. Time is too valuable to blink at infidelity. You are worth more than partiality.

Stop ignoring the signs because you think you may not find another. Stop alternating your thoughts about the signs because you think this is the best you are going to get. Stop dismissing the signs because you fear the future. Stop resisting the signs because you have found comfort. Stop blinking when you see the signs and start making decisions that will benefit your future.

Chapter 8

WHAT'S MINE IS MINE

A wise woman builds her house; a foolish
woman tears hers down with her own hands.
—Proverbs 14:1 NLT

In a dating relationship a woman wants the comfort of a man
to lie next to her at night, but sometimes this is not healthy.
Cohabitating has its place, time and season. Cohabitating early in
a relationship will send mixed signals mainly when you are trying
to understand an individual. Sometimes cohabitating early in a
relationship can lead to one taking advantage of another. Two is
better than one when you are married.

There are several states that do honor common-law marriages,
meaning that you can cohabitate without a marriage license and
reap the benefits of a married couple. Never let him/her spend
the night! He/she will not go back home to his/her roommate or
mother if he/she spends the night. This could be the beginning

of a controlling and possessive relationship. To make it to the bedroom is a no-no!

This is a note for the single independent females, the toothbrush is the first item to remain in your house, especially if he is single and does not live alone. Several articles of clothing will remain at your house the next time he spends the night. Then when you are not planning for a roommate, you will have successfully gained one without a written contract or house rules. All it takes is one or two nights to gain access to your safe haven, and then the game begins. You have taken a role you were not prepared for and have accepted responsibility you could not afford.

If you are single with your own house or apartment, treat it as a prized possession. Sometimes it may get lonely, and you may desire the comfort of a man. Stop and think about whether or not you are lost in emotion, whether you can afford another person as a responsibility or not. If he is not employed, where would half the rent come from? What if there is not enough income to substantially meet the mortgage or the rent? Ask questions, stop blinking, and remember what's yours is yours.

Serious couples in a relationship go together and look for a residence that is compatible for both styles. The only exception to this rule is when there is a family estate that has been willed to one or the other and the couple has agreed that a move there is economically feasible. Imposing on someone is rude and shows signs of desperation, immaturity, and irresponsibility. If you are not serious about the relationship, then do not let the person spend the night at your house. Your bedroom should be sacred and should have limitations.

Remember that whatever you begin the relationship with, you have to continue it in the marriage. When you chose not to continue what you started, this is where frustration and anger enters. If you started with sexual intercourse on the first date, then this is what is expected on every date. This is probably a good reason why you are going out on dates regularly. It is very important to treasure your independence until the day your spirit is released for marriage. Until then, keep your property sacred.

People do what you allow them to get away with. For example, at my home church the pastor often have picnics and dinners after service. There is a certain group of people that goes into the fellowship hall to help prepare the food, but these same people are packing plates and sodas in their cars, while the rest of the congregation remains in the service. Everyone whispers about what the certain group is doing, but no one will confront the certain group and tell them what they are doing is stealing and that this activity should cease. If the pastor or some respectable leader of the church would confront them, then this activity would stop.

This applies to relationships as well. If you see your partner using drugs and it bothers you, confront your partner. If you hear your partner swearing and saying profane words and it bothers you, have a calm and decent conversation about what you heard. Your peace of mind is at stake. If you caught a thief stealing from your house, I am sure you would call the police, identify the thief, and demand that the individual is caught and jailed.

It is called trespassing when someone invades your property. It is also called trespassing when someone comes into your home without your permission and begins settling. It is called theft when a man takes your vehicle keys off the counter and begins driving your vehicle as his own. I have heard these stories countless times from women how they started with one date but the partner moved in by the third date, without providing any financial assistance. Keep your living quarters separate and sacred if not then what is yours becomes theirs.

When you become married, this terminology is no longer in your vocabulary. It then becomes what was mine is now yours. Only maintain a selfish and independent attitude while you are single. This will help keep you focused. Remember to give God the praise for your accomplishments as a single person.

Beware of those who will try to verbally abuse you for being independent and successful. It is known as jealousy. If you are dating someone who speaks negatively about your independence and success, then keep moving. Because of your independence and success, you will need someone who will embrace you and partner with your dreams, goals, and visions to accomplish so much more. Therefore, do not blink when you hear statements such as this one: "There is no room for me here." If people are intimidated by you, they don't deserve you.

The appropriate response should be this: "Perhaps if you feel that way, then there is no room here for you." We should look for strong partners who will build a legacy with us. We should expect dreamers and visionaries for our spouses, not thugs and escaped convicts. It may take several dates before you finally meet your soul mate, but do not settle. Settling for less is not an option. Not settling while dating will save you much heartache and pain.

I would like to share a story with you about a woman named Abigail (1 Samuel 25). Abigail was married to a man named Na'bal. Abigail was intelligent and beautiful, but she married a man who was evil. Even his name suggested he was foolish. Abigail knew that her husband's foolishness may eventually cause trouble for her and her household, so she involved herself in the affairs of the business. Because she involved herself in the affairs of the business, she was informed by the workers about pertinent matters that could affect the business or the household.

One day a young man came to Abigail to inform her that her husband, Na'bal, had insulted David by not giving him the sheep he requested in exchange for his protection while they were living in the wilderness. The Scripture states, "Na'bal railed on them," meaning he complained and treated them abusively. The servant told Abigail that her husband was not a man you could speak with concerning his actions against David, which is why the servant came to Abigail. He came to Abigail because he knew that she was sensible and had good understanding. He also knew that Abigail would correct the problem.

Abigail understood that the actions of her husband would bring forth fatal consequences to her as well. Therefore, she intervened at the appropriate time. Abigail knew her husband. Therefore, she believed the report given by the worker and made the appropriate decision to make peace with David. Her action suggests that this was probably not Na'bal's first time insulting or offending God's elect. Na'bal is an example of a man you do not want to marry, but if you do marry a man of his characteristics, know that you will have to be involved in the affairs of the business to maintain peace and integrity. Abigail could have become angry with Na'bal and complained, but she did not complain; however, she reacted swiftly to the accusations.

She quickly prepared five sheep and packed loaves of bread, bottles of wine, corn, raisins, and figs for David as a peace offering on behalf of her husband, Na'bal. David accepted her prayer and her peace offering. Abigail could not risk the destruction of everything they had worked hard to accomplish because of her husband's proud and arrogant nature. After Na'bal's death David married Abigail. He knew she was a smart and humble woman, a visionary, and an intercessor.

She turned something negative into something positive. A woman harboring bitterness, hatred, anger, or unforgiveness is not emotionally stable enough to react the way Abigail reacted to save her household and her business. Not becoming involved does not bring closure to a chaotic matter. It only creates confusion. Abigail used wisdom in how she approached David as well. First she showed humility by bowing and lying prostrate before David. Second she apologized. Third she offered forgiveness.

She used information she knew about David to charm him, thus causing David to bless her and proclaim her to be a woman of good sense. Abigail understood her role as help meet and partner. Abigail accepted her vocation as a help meet and partner. She understood authority and prayer. She also knew that if she did not act expeditiously in wisdom, everything they (Abigail and Na'bal) had worked so hard to accomplish would be destroyed by the next morning.

Chapter 9

THE SAME THANG IT TOOK

He who finds a good thing, and
obtains favor from the Lord.
—Proverbs 18:22 NRSV

I began writing chapter 9 before I wrote chapters 7 and 8 because this chapter was very important for me as a minister and a single woman. I remember a year before I got "for-real saved," I was dating a guy while I was living in a metropolitan area. (I will expound on "for-real saved" in chapter 10.) This was probably my third serious relationship, and he decided we should watch a flick, as he called it, but in today's era it is called porn (pornography). After we finished watching the movie, I remember asking, "I hope you don't think I am about to do what was in that movie." Our relationship did not last long at all and ended by him telling me that he wanted to live the fast life and that I did not give him that type of freedom.

I met a young lady while I was in graduate school who was younger than I, but she knew the streets, the games, and the lingo as if she was in her forties. She made me look like the Virgin Mary. Well, I told her what the guy did and what he said, and she told me he was looking for a freak and not a wife. She said, "Wives don't do what freaks do, and if they do, they are reformed freaks turned into wives." I am glad I did not experiment with that guy by doing the things in that movie because I could not have continued that lifestyle if I became his wife.

What we fail to understand is that the same thing you do to keep the fire burning in the relationship is the same thing and more to keep the fire burning in the marriage. If not, Mr. Right or Mr. Wrong will go looking in the streets for that fire you once had, and that creates problems in any relationship. Pornography does not keep a fire burning in a marriage. Pornography creates competition in the marriage. No women should have to feel as if they need to compete with the actresses on a porn tape.

Having been married and single before marriage, I knew what I was and was not going to do in the bedroom. I understood that the Holy Scripture said the bed was undefiled and that everyone had their interpretation of what that meant. I have heard statements that the Bible means there are no limits in the bedroom. I thought it was strange for the author of Hebrews, even if the author was a single man, to write that statement, as it was never documented that he was ever married. Yet, it was stated that the marriage bed was undefiled. Who's to say the Scripture did not mean husbands should not cheat on your wives or wives should not cheat on their husbands. Perhaps if one does, the bed becomes defiled. There is so much to take and add to that one Scripture that it leads to confusion.

All I know is that it will take the same *thang* to keep a man as it did to get him to the altar. Likewise, it will take the same *thang* to keep her as it did to get her to the altar. Eventually the lies, deception, and the perpetrating will have to end, and the truth will prevail. There are some who are good at what they do, so you have to be on your best mental alert to keep in tune with what is going on.

I have been approached by married men who state the same theme. "My wife is always tired and doesn't want to be touched. My wife is ill and is mean to me. My wife this. My wife that." I wonder what my ex-husband said to women who cheated with him would say to another woman about our marriage. Married men approach me with these statements as if these are trump cards to get me to commit adultery with them. Actually these statements are repulsive and make me sick to my stomach.

Most men who approach me are cautious and most of the men who approach me I have met at some point in my life. The sad and sickening part of it all is that they are aware that I am a minister and there is a possibility that I may know their wives. It does not matter if I know their wives or not, I would not have an extramarital affair with someone's husband. But the idea of disrespecting me and the office I hold is unbelievable. I shake my head in disbelief as I write this because television condones adultery.

I remember a time when men would be afraid to approach me, but after I got married and divorced, they came from every walk of life. My girlfriend told me to expect that because I was a single woman with a little girl. She told me that to a man, this signifies that I am in need financially. They can benefit me financially, and I can benefit them sexually. This is demeaning if someone thinks that a single woman with a child is in need financially and a married man with finances is a single woman's great financial hope. A married man should be his wife's great hope financially, mentally, spiritually, and sexually.

The lingerie and the sexy songs to set the mood are still in demand once you say, "I do." Men have the dating role down to a science. When men take a woman on a date they are wearing strong cologne, have fresh breath, and are wearing neatly pressed clothing. However, when men say, "I do," they forget to freshen their breath and take baths before bed. Not all men do this once they get married, and not all women forget to purchase lingerie when they get married; however, many from both sexes do. The best thing to do is to wait until marriage before you begin experimenting with each other.

I remember hearing when I was in theology school, "Eat the meat and spit out the bones." If this book is not for you, then pass it on. If it is for you, take notes and make a change in your life. If this chapter is not for you, then move to the next chapter. This is the same for life. We learn from all our experiences.

This is my experience, and I just happened to write it in a manuscript and share it with others who do not want to experience the pain and heartache I experienced. Jay-Jay wined and dined me every Friday and Saturday night while we dated. Through the week I received roses or beautiful flowers. There was not a day when the florist was not delivering a gift to me and not a minute that passed when I did not receive a phone call or a text from him. These things quickly diminished six months into the marriage.

I would bring this to his attention, and it would change for a couple of months. Then it went back to the same neglect as before. Marriage takes consistency and intimacy. If you are acting/performing, then marriage may not be for you because marriage takes work. On the other hand, if you are genuine and want commitment, then marriage is for you. Marriage is not a short-term performance with options in the back of your mind, not if you want things to work successfully and have longevity. Some marriages will not work, even if you keep the *thang* up.

Marriage has to have God and involve the things of God. If you lose who you are and what you stand for, then the marriage is lost. Having God in your heart and in your life brings stability to a marriage. Knowing that God is the center of your marriage does not mean that Satan will not come with trials and tribulations to test your marriage. God is love (1 John 4:7 KJV). Therefore, with love and God in your heart, you can beat the adversity and fiery darts that will come.

Chapter 10

PRAY WITHOUT CEASING

Don't worry about anything; instead, pray
about everything. Tell God what you need,
and thank him for all he has done.
—Philippians 4:6 NLT

When you meet a new person, it is always good to go to God in prayer and pray for that person. Ask God the reason why you met that person. Sometimes God allow divine appointments and introductions for spiritual relationships. Often times a spiritual relationship may lead to a committed relationship. But not all relationships are committed or spiritual relationships. Prayer is essential to any relationship, therefore, I suggest praying before starting new relationships. The word relationship is very important to God and marriage. Relationship signifies unity and covenant.

A good question to ask that person is this: How is your relationship with God? This is not a comfortable question to someone who is out of fellowship with God. When one is in a relationship with a significant other, the individual is careful not to offend the other person. One also takes time to get to know that person and learn his or her likes and dislikes. This scenario is the same with God.

Because you are in fellowship with God, God will make sure you are heard and your prayers and questions are answered. Therefore, because of your relationship with God, you will receive viable information and sometimes prophetic information. Having a relationship with God is not just for ministers; however, a relationship with God is available to every human being. It is your heart that God is concerned about, and God is the only person who can see your heart, which is why it is important to consult God about forming human/physical relationships. God is a spirit, which is why our relationship with God is spiritual.

In chapter 9, I referred to myself as being "for-real saved" at one point in my life. I use this term for a lack of a better term. I would tell my students that there were three types of saved people in the world. I have been all three types in my lifetime, and I have met all three types as well. The three types include the following: (1) for-real saved, (2) borderline saved, and (3) saved.

A for-real saved person epitomizes the biblical characters Job and Anna. Job offered sacrifices to God daily on behalf of himself, his family, and his servants for fear that they had sinned against God (Job 1:5 NLT). Anna did not remarry after she lost her husband and remained in the temple to pray until the Messiah was born (Luke 2:36–37). These two characters depict for-real saved people. For-real saved people have the fear of God in their lives and they will not play with God and will present their bodies as living sacrifices to God, holy and acceptable. When I was for-real saved, I would hear God speaking as if He was sitting on my shoulders. Because I could hear God speaking clearly, I would speak about current events into a person's life that only they and God would know.

While writing this book, I realized that I must return fully to the for-real saved person and cry aloud and spare not so that God's people could be saved from damnation (Isaiah 58:1). My marriage and my divorce could have been avoided had I heeded the voice of God and stayed in tune with the things of God. I may not understand how God and marriage work, but I do know in a marriage someone has to keep praying and not give up. I stopped praying for God to prosper the marriage and to make us a loving couple, and I started praying to God with the question why. The faults and failures were amplified in my prayers instead of the legal decrees and the summons.

There is no blame in a failed marriage or a divorce. We are humans, and we make mistakes; however, it takes strong and willing individuals to put aside their pride and egos and admit the mistakes and move on. Someone in the relationship has to step up and say, "We are not going to remember the past. We will move forward." I strongly believe marriage is about legacy and teamwork. I believe marriage is working as a team to live prosperously, fulfilling lives and leaving a legacy behind once you have departed this earthly life.

I was angry and bitter with myself and carried hatred in my heart for Jay-Jay for three years. I cried bitterly to God because I did not want to forgive. In my moments of anger I knew that a lack of forgiveness brought sicknesses and hindered blessings from flowing, but I felt it was something I needed to hold against him. The thing I thought I was holding against him was being held against me. When I forgave Jay-Jay, I began writing this book, and it began to flow with ease. Doors of opportunity began to open, and the favor of God was released.

I never knew I could harbor so much hatred towards a person and still proclaim the Gospel of Jesus to others. This is when you know you have a redemptive God who has redeemed you and forgiven you even in your mess. God is a loving and gracious God. I want to take this moment and say thanks to God for forgiving me. Forgiveness is the best act of love and kindness you can give anyone, especially yourself.

The second type is borderline saved. Borderline saved reminds me of the parable in the Gospel of Luke (Luke 18) when the publican would not lift his eyes to heaven and spoke under his breath, asking God to have mercy on him. When you are borderline saved, you realize there is a God and you need God, but the things of the world are very tempting right now. In addition to being borderline saved, these borderline saved people make sure they attend the holiday worship services and funerals of loved ones, and they pray when something convicts them. Borderline saved people will not play with God and will tell someone they would rather stay in the world than be hypocrites. Borderline saved persons want a made-up mind before they start professing Jesus Christ as Lord and Savior.

Borderline saved people do not spread gossip but will see church folk participating in gossip, adulterous affairs and will not scandalize; however, they will say that behavior is the reason they do not go to church. Borderline saved people have good hearts, but they have a hard time trusting saved people because they are not sure who is real and who is phony. They know the lifestyles they are living are not in line with the Word of God, but they live them anyway. These are people who need to see true worshippers and experience the awesome power of God. I favor for-real saved people because the for-real saved people were once borderline saved people.

The third type is saved. These are the "once saved, always saved" people. These are the people the borderline saved people witness as having adulterous affairs, which cause borderline saved people to stray from the church. They are saved because they have confessed and they believe. Many of them have been baptized with water.

I am not giving you my three types of saved people to be critical or judgmental of anyone's relationship with Christ. I am certainly not a judge, and I certainly have no heaven or hell to send anyone to. This has been my observation, and I am sharing with you how I derived at these types three of people. Prayer is essential in a relationship regardless of your denomination or your spirituality. The old adage states, "Prayer is the key, and faith unlocks the door," and this is true in relationships.

Do not stop praying, even if someone makes you angry or belittles you. Keep praying even when you do not feel like praying. Keep praying! Declare revelation over your mind and ask God for spiritual eyes to see those things you cannot see with natural eyes. Consistency is good when you are praying.

Keep praying. Pray without ceasing (1 Thessalonians 5:17 KJV). Do not stop praying when the cares of life weigh you down. Do not stop praying when it seems your prayers are not being heard. That is only the trick of the Enemy because God hears your prayers. Seek God for the power of the Holy Spirit. Pray boldly and pray with expectancy.

Most importantly, fast and praise God while you are praying. Fasting clears the clutter from your mind. As a single woman, I would fast three times a week and stay in an atmosphere of praise and worship. As a married woman, this can be very difficult to do because of the demands of motherhood and spousal needs. Stay humbled regardless of how the Holy Spirit speaks and reveals things to you during your prayer time.

AFTERWORD

Marriage has to begin with a relationship with God. It does not matter where I have traveled or who I have encountered. People are having relationship issues. The issue may stem from a broken marriage or a hurtful relationship. We are all made with emotions and feelings no matter where we come from. Relationships can bring out the best or the worst in people.

My situation may not be like the next person's, but it was my learning experience. My story may not compare to the next person's story, but it may help someone. My issue may not be like the woman at the well (John 4); however, God sees my issue of loneliness, rejection, abandonment, etc., and God will free me from it. My issues have to be confronted so that healing and forgiveness may begin. It is difficult to forgive someone who has harmed or wronged us, but we must forgive so that we may be forgiven.

It takes the love of God and the work of Christ on the cross to forgive. Forgiveness only hurts the person harboring the unforgiveness. Harboring unforgiveness makes you tired, and it urges you to say ugly and mean things without realizing it.

Harboring unforgiveness does not lessen your pain. It magnifies your anger and your pride.

During the time of my broken relationship I was harboring bitterness and unforgiveness. I was emotional and irate. I did not give thought to any conversation. Whatever I thought came out. Some of my thoughts were mean and rude, but my emotions were in charge of the conversation. I wanted people to see I was the good person and my ex-husband was the bad person.

I wanted everyone to know my pain and my hurt, but it was masked with a pretty smile and cute clothes. However, my conversation revealed the hurt and the pain I bore on the inside. It is true what people say. "Hurt people hurt people." I did not use discretion in my conversations because I was trying to defend myself to the public, which really did not care either way. Hurt and unforgiveness makes you defensive.

I really believe unforgiveness brings a stench to the nostrils of God. Most divorces do not leave either party in a forgiving mood. Divorce displays the worse and best of a person. I believe this is why God hates divorce. It places the weaknesses of God's children on display. During the divorce proceedings an elected or appointed judge acts as God to determine if either party deserves certain properties acquired during the marriage.

It would behoove the couple to amicably settle the property and their differences before they both hire costly attorneys who will prolong the divorce hearings only to reap maximum benefits. If there are no financial assets to gain, then your case may be placed at the bottom of the stack. Money is priority for attorneys. An attorney has to live, eat, and work just as you and I do. Therefore, someone has to pay for the lifestyle. It is not rocket science. The plan is to allow two emotionally charged married people to take care of the pricey attorney fees.

Amicable and forgiving couples receive their divorce timely and at half the cost. It is the angry and vindictive couples who have to pay for the lifestyle of the attorney. I have friends who are attorneys and could not understand why it took six years for me to be divorced. They tried to intervene, but nothing happened and time moved on. I believe God hates divorce because of the courtroom drama and the theatrics that are involved.

Faithlessness is the root of divorce—not having enough faith in God to stay with the difficult spouse, not having enough faith in God to see what the end result will be. Having faith made Abraham righteous (Hebrews 11). Having faith the size of a mustard seed can take you places only God can take you.

I am so glad for my attorney friend who gave me the pep talk. I do not want to be that woman who opens her home to any man because I want a dad for my daughter. There are so many women who are opening their homes to various men, hoping that maybe certain ones may serve as the daddies for their children. If you know these people, give them the pep talk. The fairy tale ends here.

These are the ten proverbs I wish I had known before I got married. I hope these ten proverbs will help you before you get married or get divorced. Use this book as a journal to take your personal notes. Writing your thoughts and notes down will enhance your perception and give you spiritual discernment as it relates to potential mates. Stay committed to God. Do not stray from God if you should meet someone. This is the time to pray more.

THE PEP TALK

As a single parent, I desire my child's dad in her life, but I realize that I missed the earthly mark of selecting the right mate to be a father to my child. I did not miss the mark when I was establishing a relationship with God and teaching my child about God. My attorney friend had a heart-to-heart talk with me about letting go. I let go of my husband, but I did not let go of desiring a dad for my daughter. I want so badly for her to have her dad active in her life, but the reality is that it will not happen.

It will not happen because her dad has exhibited lack of fatherhood patterns with his older children. Therefore, it is evident he will do the same with his younger daughter. I had to let go of the idea that my daughter will have her biological father as part of her life. My attorney friend made it clear to me when she said, "My ex-husband doesn't pay child support and has no intentions of paying child support." She reminded me of how my ex-husband called me the day after my daughter's birthday to complain about how horrible of a woman I was.

My ex-husband did not call my daughter to wish her a happy birthday because he had forgotten about her birthday. However, he remembered to call me to belittle and degrade me. I stopped answering his phone calls and his text messages because he became very obscene and vulgar. My attorney friend reminded me of how these are tricks for him to generate more affidavits for my future arrests. This relationship is unhealthy, and it is not benefiting me as a human being or as a child of God.

If the relationship is unhealthy for you, then it is probably unhealthy for your child as well. It is not a good thing that a father will not provide for a child, but how much more will your heavenly father provide for His children (Matthew 6:30 KJV)? Whatever the earthly father lacks the heavenly Father will give abundantly more than you could ever ask, think, or imagine (Ephesians 3:20 KJV). Our children become a priority while they are still in our womb. Mothers are naturally nurturers. We do not want to miss any important detail of our children's lives, even if it means holding on to deadbeat dads.

As nurturers, we have to let go of the deadbeat dad. No one can make a person do something they do not want to do. The same thing applies to my daughter's dad. As mothers, we instantly know to take care of the fetus, the infant, the toddler, etc. However, the same nurturing process does not apply to the deadbeat dad. Our children deserve us. Therefore, do not hold on to deadbeat dads, expecting them to be fathers to your children because they are and will not be fathers to your children.

If the deadbeat dad has moved on with another woman and provides and cares for her children that are not biologically his children, do not be angry. I have heard stories of men providing for other men's families while their own families are struggling to make ends meet. Technically these men should provide for their partner's children as if those kids are their own biological children, but the men should also provide for their biological children as well. It hurts. But know that God is your ultimate provider and you do not have the power to change that situation. As I stated earlier, I do not understand men, and I do not know if I ever will; however, I do understand that God is a provider and will take care of you.

Be selective when you are accepting a mate or a spouse because your life and your child's life will depend on this choice. Do not hold on to a man, hoping that he will be a real dad to your child when God is available at any time to take over the role of fatherhood. Having a warm male body in the home benefits no one, but having a warm male body that is disciplining, providing for, and teaching your child benefits everyone. It hurts when I minister to high school students and they share with me that their dads get drunk and beat them until the dad passes out. Those men are unhappy people who are dealing with rejection and other unresolved issues and should not be in the same house with children.

Marriage is real. There is no prince on a white horse who will come to rescue you. It sounds good, but it is all a fairy tale. Allow the Holy Spirit to guide you in everything you do. Do not allow emotions and bitterness to dictate your future.

Forgive the person who has harmed or wronged you. Forgiving the person who has hurt you is a gift that only you can give. It is a gift of redemption and reconciliation. Yes, it hurts, and it is hard to forgive; however, you should always try. Forgiveness is a personal act to show God that you trust and believe that God's Word is true.

Prayer Journal

These are prayers I wrote during my prayer time with God. I hope you see the same manifestation of the Holy Spirit as I saw when I prayed these prayers. These prayers are filled with biblical Scriptures and the Word of God.

Day 1

Heavenly Father, help me to understand wisdom with an open heart. I will speak of excellent things and the opening of my lips shall be right things for my mouth shall speak truth. All the words of my mouth are in righteousness. There is nothing forward or perverse in my mouth (Proverbs 8:8).

Notes _____

_____

_____

_____

Day 2

Give me wisdom, dear Lord, and the knowledge of witty inventions. Riches and honor are with me. Yea double riches and righteousness. My fruit is better than gold. I lead in the way of righteousness. I may cause those that love me to inherit substance, and I will fill their treasures. I will find God. I will find life and obtain favor. Thank You, Lord (Proverbs 8:18).

Notes _____

_____

_____

_____

Day 3

Lord, give me a sharp mind. Fill me with divine knowledge and understanding. Give me the gifts to interpret dreams, explain riddles, and solve difficult problems. Lord, give me the spirit to be filled with insight, understanding, and wisdom. Keep me from sinning and help me do what is right. I break from my wicked past, and Lord, please find me innocent in Your sight. Lord, I trust in You. I do not ask because I deserve anything but because you are so merciful. Lord, we have rebelled against You and scorned Your commands and regulations (Daniel 1:17).

_____

_____

_____

Day 4

Lord, I confess my sins. I missed Your mark, Lord. I have done wrong. Lord, I repent and ask for Your help. Lord, I ask for forgiveness, and I humble myself before You. Protect me and my child. Send Your angels to protect and defend us. Heal us. In Jesus' name. Amen. (Psalm 32:5)

Notes _____

_____

_____

_____

Day 5

Father, in the name of Jesus, I bind all negative words and curses spoken about me and against me. I am not who they say I am. I am who You say I am. Lord, I release Your spirit to bless me through the Holy Spirit. In Jesus' name. Amen. (Luke 6:28)

Notes _____

_____

_____

_____

Day 6

Father, I pray for my child. I pray she or he will be great in the eyes of the Lord. She or he must not touch wine or hard liquor or drugs. She or he will be filled with the Holy Spirit even before birth. She or he will possess the power of Elijah, the prophet of old, and the spirit of the Holy Ghost. In Jesus' name. Amen (Luke 1:15).

Notes _____

_____

_____

_____

Day 7

Father, forgive me for not submitting to You and not believing that You will not leave or forsake me. Forgive me for lusting after money, material goods, food, men, clothing, houses, and cars. I confess, and I repent. In the name of Jesus. Amen (Hebrews 13:5).

Notes _____

_____

_____

_____

Day 8

Lord, I need to be honest. I feel You have left me. I feel like when I was single I was closer to You. Now I feel You are not near me. Where did I fail You? I miss You. Amen (Psalm 51:11).

Notes _____

_____

_____

_____

Day 9

God's love sounds cliché to many, but I know You love us. You love us in the midst of all chaos. You love us when tragedy comes, and You love us when trials and tribulations come. Your love is forever present. Come into my heart once more. I need You, and I desire You. In Jesus' name. Amen (John 3:16).

Notes _____

_____

_____

_____

Day 10

Lord, I come in the name of Jesus, rebuking and renouncing the worldly weapons spoken to attack Your elder, Your servant, Your son/daughter with God's mighty weapons. I break down every proud argument, particularly those that keep people from knowing God. I come against rebellious ideas and a reprobate mind. In Jesus' name. Amen (2 Corinthians 10:4).

Notes _____

_____

_____

_____

Day 11

Lord, You are faithful, and Your love endures forever. Forgive me of my sins. I repent, and I am in need of Your cleansing. Deliver me from evil, anger, and rage. Amen (1 Chronicles 16:34).

Notes _____

_____

_____

_____

Day 12

Lord, do not let any of Your words fall to the ground. You were with Samuel. Lord, be with me and my child like You were with Samuel and do not let any of her words spoken fall to the ground. Lord, appear unto me and my child in this house by the Word of the Lord. Amen (1 Samuel 3:19).

Notes _____

_____

_____

_____

Day 13

Father in heaven, in Jesus's name, I ask Your forgiveness for holding unforgiveness against my husband/wife. Lord, I know I cannot forgive him in my own strength, but by Your spirit. I have already failed, but before You now I release anger from my heart. I forgive him. Amen (Mark 11:26).

Notes _____

_____

_____

_____

Day 14

Lord, I confess that I have been unfaithful to You. Oh, God, I have cheated on You with my lusts and immorality. I need Your help to free me from my lusts. I now make a covenant with You, my Lord, to end my foolish lifestyle and start a new and committed relationship with You. I will cooperate fully in setting things in order with You, O Lord. I will follow the advice given by You and through the Holy Spirit. I will obey the laws of the land, and I will obey Your laws. Bless me indeed (Psalm 105:45).

Notes _____

_____

_____

_____

Day 15

O Lord, I know You are with me to succeed in everything I do. I know and recognize, Lord, that I am a favored woman! Thank You for blessing me. In Jesus' name. Amen (Luke 1:28).

Notes _____

_____

_____

_____

Day 16

Lord, forgive the trespass of Your servant. Since you, oh Lord, has kept me from murdering and taking vengeance into my own hands, let all mine enemies be as cursed as Abel of Maon. Please forgive me, Lord, if I have offended You and forgive those who have offended me. The Lord will surely reward me with a long and lasting dynasty, for I am fighting the Lord's battles. I have not done wrong throughout my entire life, and the blood of Jesus has covered me and washed away my sins. Even when I am chased by those who seek my life, You have secured me in Your treasure pouch, oh Lord. Now Lord, do all that You have promised me. Help me not to let anger, rage, or hatred be a blemish on my record. Then my conscience will be clear. Thank You, Lord. Amen (1 Samuel 25:26–31).

Notes _____

_____

_____

_____

Day 17

Lord, I will not be afraid of people's scorn or their slanderous talk. The moth will destroy them as it destroys clothing. The worm will eat away at them as it eats wool. But Your righteousness will last forever. This is a call to trust You, Lord. I surrender. Amen (Isaiah 51:8).

_____

_____

_____

Day 18

Lord, I feel a release in my spirit. Lord, You have taken away the cup of fury fear, dread, and desolation from my hands. Lord, thank You for giving the cup to my tormentors, who trampled me into the dust and walked on my back. Holy Spirit, keep me free from fear, dread, and desolation. Amen (Isaiah 51:17).

Notes _____

_____

_____

_____

Day 19

O Lord, please do not let my prayers and gifts to the poor and charity go unnoticed by You! Thank You, Lord, for showing no partiality. Accept me as your daughter/son. I fear You and do what is right. I know that God anointed Jesus of Nazareth with the Holy Spirit and with power. Give me the anointing to do good and to heal all those who are oppressed by the Devil. I want people to know God is with me. I ask for the power of the Lord to be upon me. I ask for God's favor and to be full of the Holy Spirit and strong in faith. Amen (Acts 10).

Notes _____

_____

_____

_____

Day 20

I will not follow a multitude to do evil; neither shall thou speak in haste. I will bring the first of the first fruits of thy land into the house of the Lord, thy God. Thank You for sending an angel before thee to keep me in the way and to bring me into the place that you have prepared. I will beware of You, God, and I will obey Your voice. When I serve You wholeheartedly, my God, bless my water and take away sickness from my midst. Drive my enemy out until Thou be increased and inherit the land. Refine me and guide me. Amen (Exodus 23:20, John 5, and Deuteronomy 26:10).

Notes _____

_____

_____

_____

Day 21

Lord, I pray for special insight into Your plans for my life. Holy Spirit, I ask for inside information on my life. Thank You for flowing within me. In Jesus' name. Amen (Jeremiah 29:11).

Notes _____

_____

_____

_____

Day 22

Lord, as you gave unto your children, including Daniel (Belteshazzar), Shadrach (Hananiah), Meshach (Mishael), Abednego (Azariah) knowledge and skill in all learning and wisdom, and Daniel understanding in all visions and dreams, I request the same understanding for myself and my family. Thank You, Lord, that Your blessings are running after me to pursue and overtake me. Amen (Daniel 5:12).

Notes _____

_____

_____

_____

Day 23

Lord, where is my Zarephath? Oh Lord, hear my voice, hear the voice of my cry and petitions. Oh Lord, let thy word in my mouth be truth. God is my source. Lord, place hedge about me and my house and about all that I have on every side and bless the work of my hands and increase my substance in the land. Amen (1 Kings 17:8).

Notes _____

_____

_____

_____

Day 24

Lord, You are good, and Your mercy endureth forever. People from every nation and tongue from generation to generation worship You because You are awesome. Thank You for this day. Forgive me and remove all malice, bitterness, and anger from my heart. Remove those judgmental thoughts about people because these thoughts would hinder me from moving forward in all You have for me to do in Your name. Thank You. In Jesus's name. Amen (Acts 4:25).

Notes _____

_____

_____

_____

Day 25

O Sovereign Lord, Creator of heaven and earth, the sea and everything in it, You spoke long ago by the Holy Spirit through our ancestor King David, Your servant, saying, "Did the nations rage?" Lord, make us sensitive to Your Holy Spirit. Teach us Your statues and precepts. Teach Your nation to love, honor, and adore You. Bless Your name, Lord. Amen (Psalm 21:1 & Psalm 46:6).

Notes _____

_____

_____

_____

Day 26

Lord, bless Your children just has You richly blessed Obed-edom. Obed's sons had sons with great abilities. Give Your people these same abilities and capabilities. Lord, we ask for Your presence and Your blessings in everything we do. Thank You for wisdom and guidance. In Jesus's name. Amen (2 Samuel 6:10–12 and 1 Chronicles 26:8).

Notes _____

_____

_____

_____

Day 27

Lord, thank You. I love myself. Lord, thank You. I forgive those who hurt me. Lord, thank You. I have wealth and riches in my house. Lord, thank You. I love my enemies. Lord, thank You. I have the mind of Christ. Lord, thank You. I am debt-free. Lord, thank You. I save and invest. Lord, thank You. I do not blink when I hear or see things that are uncomfortable or offensive. Lord, thank You. I obey Your voice. In Jesus' name. Amen (Psalm 112:3).

Notes _____

_____

_____

_____

Day 28

Lord Jesus, I believe by Your stripes I am healed. I need Your healing from this broken heart. My heart is hurting, and my emotions are running wild. I need Your supernatural healing to restore me and make me whole again. Forgive me for being angry. I release the healing power to be made whole in Jesus name. I acknowledge You, Holy Spirit, as the healer and restorer (1 Peter 2:24).

Notes _____

_____

_____

_____

Day 29

Lord, thank You for saving me by Your special favor because I believed. I cannot take credit for this because it is a gift from God. Lord, I ask for salvation for those who are struggling with loneliness, rejection, abandonment, abuse, and sexual immorality. Allow us to experience Your love, grace, and mercy. Allow us to experience Your purity and holiness. Thank You for saving Your people and forgiving us of our sins. In Jesus' name. Amen (Psalm 119:58).

Notes _____

_____

_____

_____

Day 30

Oh God, thank You for thirty days of renewal, manifestation, and transformation. I am blessed by Your Word, oh God. I thank You that I am free from anger, hatred, and malice. Thank You for forgiving me of my selfish heart. I now ask for Your mercy as You prepare a spouse for me. Thank You that my heart is ready and my mind is renewed. I believe in Your Spirit. Amen.

Notes _____

_____

_____

_____

NOTES

This section references the biblical scriptures
used in various chapters of the book.

Chapter 1

Ecclesiastes 10:19

Chapter 3

Habakkuk 2:2

Chapter 5

Second Timothy 2:16 NRSV

Chapter 9

First John 4:7

Chapter 10

Job 1:5

Luke 2:36–37

Isaiah 58:1

First Thessalonians 5:17

Afterword

John 4

Hebrews 11

Matthew 6:30

Ephesians 3:20

Prayer Journal

Proverbs 8:8

Proverbs 8:18

Daniel 1:17

Luke 1:15

Hebrews 13:5

First Chronicles 16:34

First Samuel 3:19

Psalm 105:45

Luke 1:28

First Samuel 25:26–31

Isaiah 51:8

Isaiah 51:17

Acts 10

Exodus 23:20

John 5

Deuteronomy 26:10

Daniel 5:12

First Kings 17:8

Acts 4:25

Second Samuel 6:10–12

First Chronicles 26:8

Psalm 112:3

First Peter 2:24